Reader Reviews on the Juggernaut App

'Insightful' **Saikat Biswas**

'Awesome read' **Nikhil Kumar**

'Touching' **Shiny Hoque**

'It's a heartening experience to go through the pages of this book. Moved to tears several times, a valiant effort by the author. Every Indian should read this book to grasp the life of our selfless soldiers. Salute to Indian soldiers' **Keshaw**

'Inspiring. Their sacrificed tomorrow is my today' **Jay Krishna**

'Very well written' **Varaprasad Reddy**

'Thanks a ton, Diksha, for this glimpse through their eyes. Beautifully written' **Rohan Sharma**

'Very well written, Ms Diksha . . . indeed you proved to be as brave as your father wanted to be, by bringing out elegantly the sentiments of all the brave and their families' **Parthiban Subramanian**

'This was really personal and heartfelt. It's nothing like anything I've ever read before. This is special!' **Neha Dwivedi**

'Insanely good' **Sachin Garg**

'It's inspiring as a mere mortal to read about the courage our men had to reclaim parts of our motherland. It's awe-inspiring and gave me goosebumps to read about the simplicity and the single-mindedness these gentlemen had to attain the objective. It's one thing to hear stories and totally another to read the letter[s] from the men who made the ultimate sacrifice' **Bhaskar Shankar**

'Must read for all Indians. The way our jawans have and [are] still sacrificing lives for our better tomorrow is very tough to understand. Our country and we are indebted to our dear armed forces' **Amitosh Kumar**

'Nicely compiled' **Kanu Sharma**

'A rare perspective from the minds of soldiers in the thick of battle' **Vivekjit Singh**

'Really good book' **Nilesh Aher**

'Loved reading' **Dikshit Jain**

'All letters depict positive thinking and patriotism of Indian soldiers . . . touching. Daughter's gratitude is palpable' **Sunitha Mukherjee**

'Flood of emotions . . . Thanks for writing' **Ankit Pandey**

'Saw the brutal struggle of our nation's heroes! **Shivam Agarwal**

'Loved this book. This book is close to my heart. Proud of all brave soldier[s]' **Sandhu**

'Every citizen of India should read this book' **Rajaram**

Letters from Kargil

The War through Our Soldiers' Eyes

Diksha Dwivedi

JUGGERNAUT BOOKS
KS House, 118 Shahpur Jat, New Delhi 110049, India

First published by Juggernaut Books 2017

ISBN 978-93-8622-843-7

Typeset in Adobe Caslon Pro by R. Ajith Kumar, New Delhi

Printed and bound at Thomson Press India Ltd

If I die in Combat Zone,
Box me up and ship me home,
Pin my medals all over my chest,
Tell my mom I did my best.

– William Timothy 'Tim' O'Brien

With love & peace,
Diksha

Contents

Welcome to My Life

In 1999, a war was fought at your doorstep. You may have barely felt a tremor of it. But in the dangerous mountain frontiers of our land, our men in uniform picked up their battered rucksacks and walked right into hell to save it from breaking loose. They were ordinary men like you and me, yet full of extraordinary courage.

I was eight years old that May, getting set to begin a fun vacation, like other Indian kids my age. But my father, fortunately or unfortunately, was one of those men called to the front lines to fight in the Kargil war against Pakistan.

Like you, I just wanted my dad to myself during the summer holidays. Instead we got only twelve hours with him. That May my mother, my sister and I had gone to see Daddy in Kheru, Srinagar, where his unit, 315 Field Regiment, was posted.

But he was given deployment orders just as we arrived. We never saw him again.

Had we known that those were the last twelve hours we would be spending with him, we would've done so much more with that time than just eating and sleeping with him before he put on his uniform early in the morning and left, forever.

Despite his cheerful exterior, he secretly regretted not seeing us for longer just as much as we did, or probably more. He wrote to Mummy:

> Even though the meeting was short, only twelve
> hours, it was really nice seeing you. I'll see you
> guys soon.

~

It was 3 July, and it had been more than a month since Daddy had been in Dras, Kargil. We had spent the rest of our holidays with our family in Siliguri, West Bengal, and were returning to Delhi from where we were going to take a bus or cab to our home in Meerut – our last family accommodation with Daddy. To our surprise, the whole family came to pick us up from the train station in Delhi.

I was told the news later that day. I remember that scene clearly. As I walked into the bedroom full of adults, I saw the shadow of loss reflected on everyone's face. I was a child, but I knew something was wrong and immediately turned to look at my mother.

She was sitting on a chair under a bright window, looking haggard. Her face was covered in her palms and her hair was uncombed. She was sitting crouched, her knees held tight against her. She looked like an abandoned child, someone I was about to feel like the very next second. That day I saw my father for the first time on TV – but it wasn't my Daddy, just his passport-sized photo displayed with pictures of other war martyrs in uniform. Since then, the closest I have come to feeling his touch is through his torn combat uniform and the black badge with his name imprinted on it in white – Major C.B. Dwivedi – in English and in Hindi.

~

The next few days passed in a blur. We were flown to Patna from Delhi and my mother's brother, also an army man, travelled with us in uniform. At the airport, we waited for Daddy, who was flying with us one last time, his body wrapped in the tricoloured flag. For the first time in our lives he was our responsibility, instead of the other way around.

We had to take him to his birthplace, Chandiha village, where his whole family would be waiting for him. Lieutenant Sanjeev Hariyal, a young officer from his regiment, assisted us, as did some reporters. In Patna we were greeted by the press and the chief minister, Lalu Prasad Yadav, and his wife Rabri Devi. The next day, we were again flown in a helicopter. This was the last leg of the journey for Daddy and us as a family of four, together.

We soon reached his village. I had never seen so many people at one place in my life. My father's five-foot-eleven-inch-long body was placed carefully in the gallery in front of his father's room. This was the last time we were going to be able to feel his skin, see his face.

I couldn't go close to him. As soon as the plastic sheet around him was unwrapped, I glimpsed his face from afar. It was covered in white powder, which made him look ghostly. Terrified, I ran to another room. That's the last memory I have of seeing my valiant father, my hero. I didn't salute him, I didn't try to stop him from being taken away; I simply found an escape. This eight-year-old coward was a soldier's daughter. I have never forgiven myself for that day. While my twelve-year-old sister was giving interviews wearing a brave face, I had run away from saying goodbye to the most important person in my life.

Soon it was time for his cremation. In the village, women were not allowed to attend it, and so we didn't. That's another thing I'll never get over – we didn't get a chance to light his pyre, because we were not given a choice. I know if my sister were asked, she would have grabbed the opportunity.

The news of his death, the media hype, Daddy's cremation . . . all of it happened in a span of three to four days, before we were left to ourselves to figure things out.

And then it began . . . the rest of our lonely lives.

My mother was thirty-three and clueless about many matters, but nothing could stop her from working towards the best future for her daughters, just as she and her loving husband had planned. In his letters he would often write to her about how she could help their older daughter Neha feel secure after I was born. He would say, 'After all, she's our first daughter.' He made sure he personally took part in our upbringing, even if it meant distance learning.

16 July 1998

My Dear Neha and Diksha,

I am fine here and hope the same with you all. I have not received any letters till date from you, but I know it is due to postal strike. Very soon I will get all your letters and you will get mine.

You know how I pass time? I pass my time thinking about you – your days when you were small kids, hardly able to walk or speak – then slowly growing and reaching where you two are today. It is nice to think about it all. If you want to revise your memory, go through the album – you will remember a lot.

How are your studies going and also the fights?

Take care and do well.
Rest in the next letter.
With love,
Your daddy.

Through his letters, he held our hand every step of the way, he taught us to create memories and hold on to them while he was away. Now Mummy had to make both Neha di and me feel safe, all on her own. In those days, you'd often find her awake at night, sitting in the drawing room, holding Daddy's framed picture close to her heart, whimpering, as if she were talking to him to make a mindful decision.

~

The victory of the Indian army in the Kargil war in 1999 was based on a foundation of four factors – courage, determination, junior leadership and destiny. Everything else worked against them – from their positioning to their timing and preparations. Had it not been for the willingness of soldiers like my father to die for their country,

Operation Vijay, as the war was also called, would not have been a success. For years I blamed my father for choosing the country over us. It is only recently that I have learnt to accept his sacrifice as a blessing.

It has been eighteen years now. His ashes have washed away and his tales of valour are forgotten. Like most of the 527 martyrs of the war, barring a few, who gave their life to the country. Over the years I would wait for someone to write about my father, but it never happened.

I had stuck Daddy's nameplate on to my noticeboard in front of my study table. From time to time, I would spend several minutes staring at it while I worked. Every time I saw it, it made me restless and angry. It made me wonder if my father's sacrifice was any less than the heroic sagas that were thrown at me every day on the Internet. That he wasn't alone in this made me even more upset. It wasn't just my father whose story was untold. There were 500 heroes from the Kargil war whose stories were yet to be told.

And so, I decided to write this book. I wanted to make you dip into the minds of those selfless men in uniform who wake up every morning so you can sleep peacefully at night. The best way to do this would be through the soldiers themselves, by using their own words and voices. With this in mind, I began to search for their letters and diaries.

Initially I was hesitant. How was I going to find their names? How was I going to get in touch with them? Would their families be pleased to hear from me? It wasn't going to be easy to make a martyr's family remember details about their son, father, husband, brother. It was like opening old wounds. Ironically, I was the one doing that. A martyr's daughter who's been through it all. Reading those letters makes you want to tear right through the eighteen years, to that fateful summer of May–July 1999, and stop them.

My visit to Kargil in July 2016 for the Kargil Vijay Diwas gave a kick-start to my research. The memorial hall in Dras reminded me of what we were really missing about the heroes of Kargil – their voices. I returned feeling energized and determined. I read every article available on the Internet about the war. Then I tried to buy some of the books written on it during that period. None of them were in stock! Eighteen years had seen a curtain fall over the war. It seemed like a forgotten event. I finally got my hands on *The Heroes of Kargil,* which was put together by Army Headquarters, and *Dateline Kargil* by Gaurav C. Sawant.

I then went to my mother for help. She is a powerhouse of contacts when it comes to the Indian army. This book wouldn't have been possible without her. Call after call, story after story, one name led to another. I got more and more names, and more and more information.

But the deeper I went, the more challenges I faced. Many of those 527 soldiers' families live in villages, without access to the Internet. It's next to impossible to reach them. There was a time when I thought of giving up, daunted by the immensity of the task.

And then I stumbled upon a letter that reminded me of the very reason why I had started the project. In that letter Daddy had called me a 'brave girl'. I felt a gush of pride, but it was immediately clouded by a sense of shame at the memory of my behaviour during his last rites. He was right – I was brave, despite my behaviour. And this was my chance, my chance to prove it.

8 July 1998

My Dear Diksha,

I am fine here and hope the same with you all.

It was nice talking to you on the phone yesterday. I know you are a brave girl and will help mummy and didi in their work. How is your ear now?

It is nice that Mausaji and Mausiji are coming to meet you all. Do call nanaji also.

I am sure, you must be preparing well for your classes.

With love,

Your daddy.

So I decided to go ahead. I reassessed my approach to this book. Instead of telling the stories of 500-plus soldiers, I would focus on a smaller cast of characters and make them come alive, narrating the story of the war through their eyes. I'd like to think that although this book does not mention every hero who sacrificed his life in the Kargil war, it represents each one of them.

The heroes of Kargil had a lot more in common than what met the eye. They talked, walked and breathed the same language and thoughts. Indeed, the letters and journal entries that I read often seemed as if they were written by one person. Their love for their country, their ties to their families, their constant efforts to protect their loved ones from feeling nervous, the absence of regret about their decisions, their complete focus – these were the distinctive preoccupations of the soldiers that come across in the letters you are about to read.

A war like the Kargil war will not be fought again. The Indian army will probably not be so surprised by and so underprepared for mountain warfare ever again. Through this book, the story of that war and its heroes will be told to you, now by me. And this time, you won't be able to forget that story, because it's the heroes themselves talking to you.

1

Dear Daddy

Dear Daddy,

It's difficult. Life is difficult. Today I'm not going to start this letter saying, 'How are you? We're fine here and hope the same with you.' Because we're not. We haven't been for eighteen years. We've only just managed to survive.

Calling you Daddy feels small. It's not how I want to address you because you're not my father first, you never were. You're an angel who touched our lives to turn it into a dream.

Even in your absence, you turned a small-town woman into a strong, independent businesswoman who learnt to support her two daughters all on her own. You turned a daughter, who didn't know how to prepare for her exams without you, into a mother to her younger sister at the age of twelve. And you turned your younger daughter into a force you could have never imagined her to be. All this, just by your memory and your words.

But I'm going to stick to calling you Daddy in this letter because it feels personal. Personal enough to make me feel like you're still here somewhere. Maybe you're sitting right next to me, looking over what I'm writing. Maybe you want to make up for all those years you didn't pay attention to my studies because Neha di's studies were more important. I have always wondered if she was your favourite daughter. Unfortunately, I'll never know.

You had always protected us from the harshness of reality. You were always a part of our life even when you weren't around. You made sure your two daughters never woke up feeling abandoned every time you had to return to your unit, 315 Field Regiment (Kargil), after your leave would end. Even when you were on duty, you held our hands, those of your three girls, every step of the way.

You left us notes full of advice and your warmth so Neha di and I didn't have to wake up missing you, or feel scared that you weren't there to help and protect us. They took us through the day, your words ringing in our minds – they were the first things we saw when we woke up and the last things we remembered as we put our sleepy heads on our pillows. They helped guide Mummy too.

On 8 June 1997, before going back to Kheru after spending your leave days with us in Meerut, you left behind these for us:

Dear Diksha,

Wake up early in the morning with a smile. Brush your teeth. Drink milk before going to school.

Pay attention in class. Have lunch and rest a while.

Play in the evening. Do your homework. Have dinner. Pray to God, before sleeping.

With best wishes,

Daddy.

Dear Neha,

Just by paying a little more attention you would be able to score very high marks.

With best wishes,

Daddy.

We began our days with your notes. We ended them with prayers for you. 'Seek what you want and chant the *gayatri mantra* twelve times before you sleep,' you told us. I followed your advice: 'Dear God, please help me score well in exams. Please take care of Daddy wherever he is and make sure they all come back safe from war. *Aum Bhur Bhuvah Swah, Tat Savitur Varenyam Bhargo Devasya Dhimahi, Dhiyo Yo Nah Prachodayat* (x12).'

Sometimes I would throw in a couple of extra selfish wishes, but our prayers always ended with, 'Take care of Daddy, please send him back home safe.' We were kids and there were times that we'd doze off without praying, but even then we would wake up with a jolt in the middle of the night, sit up, fold our hands and quickly say our prayers before going back to sleep again. We strongly believed that so long as we prayed nothing could go wrong. But just like that, God betrayed me, God betrayed us.

We were told that you spoke of us in your final moments. You had said to one of the soldiers, 'I have two daughters, Neha and Diksha . . .', but could not complete the sentence. You choked, they said, Daddy. Even on your deathbed, you knew very well that your family, your three girls, would be lost without you.

I often wonder why and how I remember you so clearly. Did some part of my subconscious self know that I was going to lose you so early in my life? That I should try and capture every moment I had with you because that's all I'd have to live with for the rest of my life? There's no other reason why I'd remember pulling a strand of hair from the back of your hand when I was three or four. I was in your lap and you jumped in pain, but no, you didn't let me fall. You never let us fall.

I remember everything. You folding one side of a sheet of paper to prepare us for 'Match the Following' for our exams, you making us ice lollies, teaching me why a donkey is called '*gadha*'. What I can't remember, however, is you getting angry. You never scolded me. I wish you had. I would be able to play it in my head, like all the other things about you, when I need to think of you.

We didn't realize other dads weren't like you, that you were an exception and not the rule. I still keep trying to find you in every man I meet. I know what they think when I tell them, 'My father was the most perfect man I've ever come across.' They assume in their heads that every daughter talks about her father like that. It's frustrating that I can't prove it to them. It's frustrating that I can't show off your chivalry, sensitivity, kindness and your unapologetic sense of humour to the world.

You, in every sense of the word, were a gentleman-officer, as gentlemanly as one can be. And, my Daddy or not, I salute you! I can promise you, Daddy, that even if I hadn't met you as your daughter, I would be in love with you.

Your greatest gift to me is the fire in my heart and the restlessness in my mind that won't allow my life to go to waste. You called me 'Pepsodent', and rightly so. Before I knew it, you knew I was made for '*dhishum dhishum*' in this big bad world. After all, I'm a hero's daughter.

With love in my heart and pride in my soul,
Yours forever,
Pepsodent.

2

The Beginning

A cold, harsh wind brushes the skin of the shivering soldier. His backpack is heavy and his stomach light. He looks forward to the next time he'll eat. He has already eaten his four puris and sabzi for the day. He's marching forward in knee-deep snow because that's what he does, that's his duty.

When his commanding officer asked him, 'How many of you are ready to die?', he raised his hand without a second thought. This soldier and countless others like him are the reason why Operation Vijay in 1999 was a success, why the Srinagar–Leh highway is safe and why Kargil district and the Siachen Glacier are parts of India today.

The mountainous landscape of Kargil lies 205 km away from Srinagar in the Ladakh region. It consists of peaks 16,000 feet to 20,000 feet high, with some of the steepest and most difficult-to-negotiate terrains known to man. The air at such levels is thin and devoid of oxygen, making it incredibly hard to survive there, let alone be active, without proper acclimatization. Underprepared soldiers had to walk for hours in these mountains to take positions, retrieve the bodies of the martyrs and try to avoid enemy fire at a short range.

This was the terrifying battlefield, a stretch of about 250 km, on which the Kargil war played out.

~

India had no reason to expect a conflict with Pakistan in 1999. The separatist activities in Kashmir, some of which were supported by Pakistan, had escalated in the 1990s. Nuclear tests had just been conducted by both India and Pakistan in 1998, ratcheting up tensions between the two countries. Across the Line of Control (LoC), both sides saw aggression, with the Pakistani side openly firing and the Indian army sending their soldiers in offensive assaults along the Marpo La ridgeline in Dras. Attacks were planned and men were sent, but good sense prevailed, and the Indian army called off the operation at the last minute. Indian soldiers even celebrated the 'no conflict' decision with whisky and Old Monk in their tents, completely unaware of what was cooking on the other side of the mountain.

The new year witnessed a more harmonious turn. Prime Minister Atal Bihari Vajpayee had initiated peace talks with Prime Minister Nawaz Sharif of Pakistan, and the Lahore Declaration was signed in February 1999 to defuse the situation. The Delhi–Lahore bus service was inaugurated that month as a gesture of goodwill. The Indo-Pak Test series, which had begun in January, was on in full swing in India – it was a series that had gripped both nations equally. Things were looking up so far as Indo-Pak relations were concerned.

The story in Kargil, however, was very different – it was, in fact, in unimaginable contrast to the apparent calm there. 3 May 1999 was a typical summer day, before local shepherds noticed a few armed men wandering about in Kargil, and reported the news to the Indian army. These men, who were carrying weapons, were dressed in salwar-kameez and appeared to be mujahideens – Kashmiri separatist militants who were fighting the Indian government.

They were, in fact, neither terrorists nor locals out on a stroll in Kargil, but Pakistani soldiers with legitimate identity cards, who had infiltrated the border with a deadly plan. Since the Indo-Pakistan war of 1971, this was the first time Pakistan had breached the 1972 Simla Agreement, in which the two countries had agreed to respect the LoC which separated them and keep peace.

It was a bold move by the Pakistani army, and it had a number of objectives.

One, they wanted to sever the Srinagar–Leh National Highway (NH 1A), which ran through Kargil district, cutting India's lifeline to Leh. Two, they wanted to choke reinforcements to Indian troops at the Saltoro ridge on the Siachen Glacier guarding the Indian side of the LoC. Three, they wanted to open a new route for infiltration into the Kashmir Valley and the Doda–Kishtwar–Bhaderwah region over the Amarnath mountain.

Four, they would have liked, if it were possible, to spread Islamic fundamentalism in Ladakh. Some experts argue that the Pakistani army took this step without a go-ahead from their prime minister.

Every year during winter, parts of the Kashmir border were left unpatrolled by both the Pakistani and Indian armies because of the inhospitable weather. By an unspoken rule, both sides trusted each other to not cross the borders during this time. However, 1999 was different.

As the weather conditions became better and the Pakistani army began to reoccupy the unheld areas on their side of the LoC, they decided to also send forces to occupy some posts on the Indian side. Soldiers from the Northern Light Infantry (NLI) of the Pakistani army, disguised in salwar-kameez, moved to establish themselves atop the high mountain ridgelines in the Mushkoh Valley, and the Dras, Kaksar and Batalik sectors. With the occupation of these areas, the Pakistani soldiers had captured every major ridgeline that was critical for the Indian army to carry out their operations in the valley.

These infiltrated areas were cordoned off with

a tall, heavy wall of sandbags called *sangars*. The Pakistani soldiers ensconced themselves within these cordons, with ample rations and heavy and light weapons. Administrative bases were built in Pakistan-occupied Kashmir to keep the channels open so that reinforcements could be provided. Additional telephone cables were laid to keep communication open with Pakistan, and plastic anti-personnel mines were dug into the ground to keep the Indian army away for as long as possible. So this was the scene – one fully equipped army lying in wait, ready to spring upon a completely ill-prepared one.

The Pakistani army did everything in their capacity to keep this operation a secret. They even refused to recognize the dead bodies of the first few Pakistani soldiers who were caught intruding on the Indian side of the LoC on 3 May 1999. Those bodies were finally cremated by the Indian army. Such were the precautions that the Pakistani army had taken. The Indian army had no clue what was about to hit them.

3

A Battle of Restraint

The beginnings of the war can be traced back to late 1998. While Indian intelligence may have failed the nation and its army, every soldier who was posted around the regions of the Mushkoh Valley, and the Dras, Kaksar and Batalik sectors in the winter of that year knew that something was wrong and that something was building up.

The hard, cold months saw repeated ceasefire violations by Pakistan. While there were disturbances across the border often, the constant firing by the Pakistanis was perhaps a way to distract the Indian army from getting wind of their larger plan. Nobody knew what these disturbances were leading to but the Indian side's patience was being tested every day. Our soldiers' hands were tied. They were desperate to take revenge for the brother-soldiers they were losing every day, but they didn't have the orders to retaliate.

They were frustrating times for every Indian soldier. One such young man was Lieutenant Amit Bhardwaj of 4 Jat, stationed in Dalunag, Kargil. His diary provides a vivid account of life on the Kargil border during those months.

Today is Dussehra and the enemy opened heavy fire exactly at 0005 hours, maybe they are in much more hurry to celebrate the festival. I am sitting in my bunker getting ready for another day of night firing. It is always the enemy that opens up fire first, and then we reply back. It is basically a battle of restraint from our side. We reply back just to show that we are alert. How much I would love to take the initiative and have a go at the enemy, but our orders are such that we do not take the first shot and only reply back. The seniors have their own policy and we have to follow their orders.

It was Amit's dream to be a 'one-man army' and fight all the evil in this world. As a young boy he'd often write in his journal that he wanted to be 'Godfather' – a powerful man that the world would one day admire and respect. It was his dream to join the army for that very reason, to make a difference with the body of steel that he had worked hard to build over many years.

Lieutenant Bhardwaj aimed for the moon, and reached it too, while fighting for the country till his last breath.

19 October 1998
2000 HOURS

Today is Diwali. The festival of light, it symbolizes the victory of truth over lies. Far away from home in these snowy mountains and bone-chilling cold, my comrades and I are safeguarding our borders from enemies. Every now and then the valley reverberates with the sound of gunfire. With feet deep in snow and alert with their guns, our soldiers are responding to each threat from the enemy with twice the intensity and vigour, but my heart is somewhere else.

An image keeps reappearing in front of my

eyes – that of the edge of my terrace brightly
lit up with diyas, firecrackers that go up in the
air and create a rainbow in the night sky, the
auspicious time of Lakshmi poojan and the
tranquillity of the hymns that silence everything
around me. All these images come to me in a
flash, and I imagine myself roaming around
carefree till the wee hours of the next day,
cosy in the love and warmth of close friends
and neighbours.

This is my third Diwali away from home.
Sitting alone in this trench, I am consoling
myself with the sense of duty that I have for my
nation. Even so, the kid that somewhere lives in a
quiet corner of my heart is getting restless to eat
that sweet from his mother's hands. Every second
moment, that face – my mother's – flashes in
front of my eyes. She would be lighting the diyas
right now, and her hands might just freeze at the
thought of her son who is guarding the nation
at the border. My father would be consoling her
and becoming emotional at the same time.

But mine is not the only mother missing
her son, there are so many other brave mothers,

whose sons are fighting with their lives on the
edge in these treacherous situations and making
sure that the enemy is not able to move a step
further. My mother at least has this consolation
that I will come home the next time I get leave
from duty. But what about my fellow comrades
Arjun and Satpal, for them the next time off
doesn't hold any meaning. They have sacrificed
their lives in service to the nation.

~

The firing intensified in the new year. Twenty-
two-year-old Lieutenant Saurabh Kalia was
commissioned on 12 December 1998. 'Today, I
am proud that I have joined 4 Jat regiment, a day
will come when this unit will be proud of me,' he
said, in the shortest speech made by anyone at
his orientation, not realizing he was speaking the
absolute truth.

Lieutenant Bhardwaj was overjoyed to have
this new young officer reporting to him. For him,
Lieutenant Kalia was the 'little kid of the *paltan*'.
He'd tell his sister often, 'Now I have a *bachcha*

who will do all the work for me, and someone who will call me sir.' He trained his junior officer to be the leader he was and felt as responsible for him as a father for his firstborn, teaching him the traditions and history of the *paltan* – when the regiment was raised, the work it had done, the laurels it had won – making him an officer proud of his regiment.

Lieutenant Kalia was inspired by his senior subaltern to record his days in a journal. His diary entry, titled 'Op Dalunag', contained a day-to-day account of what was happening in his region in early 1999, much before Operation Vijay was declared:

5 Feb 1999: Pak fired 105 mortar and arty rounds on all posts of our Bn at 1200 hrs and 1700 hrs.

6 Feb 1999: (1) We fired 10 rounds of L70 gun on Pak post. Bunker ridge from Choti post.

(2) In return Pak fired some 20 mortar and arty rounds on Choti post in coordination with some bursts from BMG.

16 Feb 1999: Kazi and saddle complex killed two Pakis with sniper rifles as too much movement was seen on Pak post.

On 14 Feb and 15 Feb '99, Pak fired two ill rounds of 2-inch mortar at 0330 hrs and 0130 hrs respectively and links were seen climbing their posts with torch by Dalunag post. In return Pak fired some 310 rnds of BMG, 48 rnds of RPG, and 10 rnds of UMG.

17 Feb 1999: Whole day Pakis were trying to bring back the body and so fired on saddle complex with mortar, arty, and automatic machine guns. They were unable to bring back the body till 1900 hrs. Their sniper was seen sitting in the rocks by saddle complex. He fired one round on 05 post but no harm was done.

From 18 February onwards, there were two to three rounds of firing every day from the 'other side', as noted by Lieutenant Kalia at the end of his journal entry.

Despite these daily skirmishes, there was no warning from intelligence. Nor had the 121

(Independent) Infantry Brigade guarding the valley succeeded in picking up the signals. The secret was finally revealed in May 1999.

4

The Big Revelation

The picture got clearer for the Indian army, one step at a time. Unaware and under-equipped, a few Indian soldiers landed on the deadly, almost suicidal, peaks of Kargil district on 5 May 1999 in response to the shepherds' report. These search parties were sent up to investigate what was assumed to be a small infiltration by mujahideens. Instead, they reported large-scale intrusions in every area they checked.

Lieutenant Saurabh Kalia's patrol was the first search party to report news of intrusion by the Pakistani army. He and his team of five soldiers – sepoys Arjun Ram, Bhanwar Lal Bagaria, Bhika Ram, Moola Ram and Naresh Singh – from 4 Jat went missing in the Batalik sector on 14 May 1999 while on their search mission.

His officer, Lieutenant Amit Bhardwaj, and

Havaldar Rajvir Singh volunteered to lead a search and rescue mission for Lieutenant Kalia's team on 17 May. Lieutenant Bhardwaj set out with a team of about thirty soldiers. Like Lieutenant Kalia must have, they too faced intense firing on their way to the Batalik sector at the Bajrang post.

The enemy had something the Indian army did not have – better positioning.

They had taken their places comfortably atop the key Kargil ridges, occupying about twenty-five kilometres of Indian territory well before the Indian soldiers were even deployed. In any high-altitude warfare, the attacker is at an obvious disadvantage to the defender. Ironically, India, on its own land, was the attacker, and Pakistan, sitting tight at their positions, the defender.

This meant that for every Pakistani soldier enjoying the gorgeous view of the blue skies and snowy peaks, ten Indian soldiers had to risk their lives to equal him in that particular fight. This also meant that every Indian officer leading his troop for the attacks was well aware that two out of ten of his men wouldn't return alive.

Lieutenant Bhardwaj immediately realized that

this was no ordinary attack, and that he and his men were outnumbered. He ordered his men to retreat and report to the base camp for help, while he would provide cover fire. But that day Havaldar Rajvir Singh couldn't find it in himself to listen to his sahab's orders, and stayed by his side. The first volley of Browning Machine Gun (BMG) burst hit Lieutenant Bhardwaj. He fought back bravely, killing ten Pakistani soldiers. Eventually running out of ammunition, he was hit twice. Even in his last moments, he continued imploring Havaldar Rajvir to join the rest of the men, but failed to convince him. In the truest tradition of Jats, the two soldiers from 4 Jat didn't leave each other's side till the end.

The Pakistani soldiers didn't let the Indian soldiers approach the place where these two brave soldiers lay dead. They were declared 'missing'.

'I believe he's still fighting out there,' said Lieutenant Bhardwaj's father, when well-wishers offered their condolences.

The two soldiers' bodies lay in the snow until they were retrieved on 13 July, fifty-six days later. Lieutenant Bhardwaj's hand was holding his weapon firmly when his body was recovered. It was evident that he had fought till his last breath.

Nearly three weeks after Lieutenant Bhardwaj's death, the bodies of Lieutenant Kalia and his team were handed over by the Pakistani soldiers to the Indian authorities. While on their search mission, Lieutenant Kalia and his troops had gotten embroiled in a crossfire with enemy forces from across the LoC, and had eventually run out of ammunition. They had finally been encircled by a platoon of Pakistani rangers and taken as prisoners of war.

The bodies were returned in a condition that would put any army in the world to shame. Vital parts were missing, eyeballs had been dug out and their noses, ears and genitals had been chopped off. They also bore several cigarette burns. It was barbarism at its worst.

Reacting to this horrific act, a military official had remarked, 'This is a gift by Pakistan to India a few days before its foreign minister Sartaj Aziz's visit to New Delhi to discuss the Kargil situation.' Pakistan's foreign minister was to arrive in New

Delhi on 12 June for 'peace talks' between the two countries.

By the time the Indian army received the bodies, the operation was at its peak. The six Indian soldiers were prisoners of war and they should not have been tortured. Pakistan had clearly breached the Geneva Convention (1929), which sets out clear rules about how soldiers must be treated if they are detained by the enemy, and emphasizes that a prisoner of war has the right to be treated with honour and respect at all times. A notice against this breach was submitted on 15 June 1999. The deputy high commissioner of the Pakistani embassy in New Delhi was summoned, but justice was not granted due to absence of sufficient proof. Lieutenant Kalia's family continues to fight.

~

Until these initial operations got under way, the Indian army didn't know that a whole army of Pakistani men was waiting to surprise them on the snowy peaks that belonged to India. As soon as this harsh reality hit them, they jumped to action, knowing that this operation needed more than just one brigade and a few hardened soldiers to reoccupy the land where the enemy was perched.

The Indian army needed to make eviction plans, and it needed offence and not defence this time. Operation Vijay was announced. Under this programme, 200,000 Indian troops were mobilized. On 17 May, the Indian army officially embarked on the operation. For the first time in many years, every service of the Indian armed forces came together to fight a battle that would be remembered for years to come.

General Ved Prakash Malik, then chief of army staff, cut short his official trip abroad to visit Kargil, and Prime Minister Atal Bihari Vajpayee declared, ' . . . it's a warlike situation,' on 31 May. The stretch of peaks and ridgelines captured by the Pakistani army was vast, with each segment lying anywhere between 4–5 km and 7–8 km. The intruders had built *sangar*s inside which they had dumped all their military stores. The Indian army divided these locations, assigning the recapture of each to specific regiments. Various regions were divided into 'points' that would then be assigned to different regiments as attack targets. This was part of their eviction plan. The Indian military strategy was to push the enemy from one point to another, from one peak to the next, forcing them to leave behind their arms and ammunition at every step.

Victory would be achieved in two ways. First, by bringing together the air force, army aviators, paramilitary forces, special forces, signalmen and engineers into a powerful functioning whole. This operation was not like tackling any other conflict; it needed weakening the enemy from all sides first, calling for a synergistic approach by all units of the defence forces.

The Pakistani soldiers had spread blankets of mines as they climbed up to the peaks they had occupied. So every step forward for an Indian foot soldier was a near-death experience. The Indians knew too that they were being watched by the enemy army who had a bird's-eye view from their position on top. That's where artillery and the second winning strategy came into the picture. Artillery assault was mandatory because the enemy had to be distracted for the infantrymen to have a chance at accomplishing their task of recapturing the land, point by point, with the least possible casualties.

This was also why scores of soldiers were sent for every single attack, because points of failure would be many until the soldier reached the battle zone. Hand-to-hand combat using the infantry was the only option for the Indian army to recapture their land without harming innocent lives. This was the hardest possible strategy – the Indian foot soldier had to navigate narrow, super high-altitude approaches under thundering fire from several directions. In fact, to avoid escalating the conflict, an internal decision was made by the Indian authorities to not cross the LoC.

~

The weeks between 5 May and 31 May were extremely tough for the Indian army. There was absolutely no information about the location of the enemy, so the artillery units had to adopt a hit-and-miss process, firing at one place and quickly moving on to another location before there could be any retaliation. All this was done in complete darkness, with the headlights of army vehicles switched off.

The first air-to-ground strikes by Fighter Ground-Attack (FGA) aircraft were launched on 26 May. While the additional troops were building up and acclimatizing to the altitude in the short span of time they had on their hands, troops were instructed to cut off all supply lines to the enemy. The Special Forces (SF) were also employed for this task. Simultaneously, the enemy was kept on edge by a continuous barrage of Harassing Fire (HF) by the artillery.

Finally, after a series of failed operations and casualties, all the ridgelines that could be used to control the national highway connecting Srinagar to Leh were cleared of the enemy by 31 May. It was then time for extensive infantry assaults.

The war really turned around in June with the recapture of the Tololing ridgeline, the dominant Indian peak that overlooked the 510-km-long Srinagar–Kargil–Leh highway. Tololing's control by the enemy was a nightmare for the Indian armed forces. The Pakistani armed forces knew what the stakes were and were prepared to hold their ground. They had had a particularly dangerous trick up their sleeve in Tololing – sophisticated electronic jammers to blank out Indian army radio sets.

The young soldiers of 2 Raj Rif (Rajputana Rifles), who were assigned the task of recapturing Tololing, were used to interruptions in radio messages and being cut off from communication on the suicidal peaks of the ridgeline. Their chances were bleak, but Tololing and its adjacent peaks had to be recaptured at any cost.

However, on the early morning of 13 June at precisely 4.10 a.m., there were no radio interruptions. From the Tololing peak, the commanding officer of 2 Raj Rif, Colonel M.B. Ravindranath, radioed the commander of 8 Mountain Division, Major General Mohinder Puri, giving him the good news, 'Sir, I'm on Tololing top.' Just minutes ago his troops had recaptured the key ridge in the Dras sector after a fierce night-long hand-to-hand battle.

The next six days saw a series of successful operations at the mountain tops adjacent to

Tololing – Point 4590, Rocky Knob, Hump and Point 5140. Many of the soldiers whose letters you will find here died in these battles. So did Daddy.

But the biggest battles won were the ones of the human spirit. Our army was fighting against all odds, not only ill-prepared but also completely ill-equipped. Unlike Pakistan, the Indian army didn't have enough time to make helipads to ensure smooth transportation of their reinforcements. So soldiers had to carry their own supply of food, water and ammunition. It could be days' or months' long supplies – the lightest rucksack was about 31 kg, and the only way to not carry more weight than that was if you left most of the food and water behind, ammunition being the number one priority for most soldiers.

> It's really difficult to fight the enemy at this altitude. He is well inside bunkers and defences and we are in the open. He has planned his move very well and has occupied most of the heights.
> – Lieutenant Praveen Tomar

Our soldiers were living like wild animals.

With one pair of clothing, without any water to drink or food to eat, they were hungry, thirsty demigods fighting in the mountains. In a place where even to defecate you needed to anchor yourself in the snow, they had to look for ways to feel human. That's when they wrote stories in their letters and diaries, telling us from ground zero of their fight for the country.

For Indian soldiers, this war was indeed the survival of the fittest, but they were only too happy for this golden opportunity to make their mark.

5

Comfort Me with Lies

Imagine waking up in the morning and sipping the last hot cup of tea with your wife and kids, before your leave ends. It is now time to be on the field again. You want to freeze that moment, capture it in your head and carry it around in your olive-green pockets, behind all the badges and medals you've earned during your service. That is the price tag placed on the job of waking up every day to protect your country.

Dying while fighting for your country or taking every step with caution to live for your loved ones is every soldier's dilemma. Major Rajesh Singh Adhikari of 18 Grenadiers had just brought his bride home, before duty called and he was forced to leave her behind. Hailing from Garhwal, where every third house is a soldier's home, Major Adhikari's mother could only pray that the next coffin to come home wasn't her son's. But his wife of ten months, Kiran, who hadn't grown up on soldiers' tales of heroism, had no reason to expect such an outcome. Major Adhikari, too, only thought of the happy future with his wonderful wife. After all, they had a lifetime ahead of them.

> Disheartened to find the STD out of order I just left it to God to give my baby the strength.
> – Major Rajesh Singh Adhikari

The excerpts from his diary bring to life one of the biggest challenges that beset the soldier's mind when he's at war. It's his golden opportunity to prove to his country his patriotism, but the trade-off is that he may not see his loved ones ever again. And that can mean he may never be the lover he wanted to be.

It was evidently a proud moment for Major Adhikari, for he and his boys were about to make history, but thoughts of his beloved never escaped his mind, even on the toughest days of his life. It didn't help that it was very hard to stay in touch with family during this time.

He wrote in his diary:

14 May 1999

The day was a continuation of the cdo operations, and as I did not have dinner last night I could feel the weakness. As officer in charge for the operations for 18 GRENADIERS I had a lot of responsibility, and when our torture finally finished at 1400 hours the encouraging words from CO 1 BIHAR (HAKA) were indeed a good medicine. Thereafter what happened is lost in my sleep.

15 May 1999

There is no feeling greater for a soldier than what comes to him before moving for war. Today as I read orders to move my coy within 24 hours to Dras, I was so amused that I couldn't stop smiling. At the same time the first thought that struck me was that what will I do to communicate with Kiran from today onwards. Anyways the prep went on and the coy log, stock, and barrel moved to 13 HQ at 1900 h. Thereafter a night busy packing, loading and other prep for war.

16 May 1999

There was no night and ready to move. I with my coy moved to Sonamarg to establish camp for the rest of the battalion. B coy did an excellent job and the party went really good.

Disheartened to find the STD out of order I just left it to God to give my baby the strength.

18 May 1999

One more order to move and the camp shifted from Matayan to Mugalpur. The organization of my coy and settling the load tables kept me busy. Thereafter the briefing by 2IC brought some relief as we would get a few days for acclimatization. However, the situation ahead and our task is still not clear. The uncertainty is one factor that irritates me the most. Anyway time was not so tense and busy ever before and the thought of me going into real war too was as never before. It's heartening to see the morale of the troops and their willingness to fight this battle. The task that we wore this uniform for is finally in our hands and it's encouraging to see everybody's willingness to do it.

In the early days of the war, the regiments were still acclimatizing at lower altitudes, where there was still scope for telephone connectivity and STD provisions. But unfortunately, there was no guarantee these would function, as Major Adhikari was to discover. No special facilities could have been provided either – the army had too little time at hand to organize anything of this sort. They barely had any satellite phones. The same phones were sometimes circulated from post to post so a soldier could contact his anxious family members and sometimes pass on messages to his fellow soldiers' families too. It was a trend at the time – communication was such a big issue that soldiers became the 'messengers of war' to each other. If any soldier got a chance to call home, he'd make sure he gave his family a list of numbers to call to inform other soldiers' families of their well-being. Such was their desperation to keep their loved ones at ease during wartime.

In fact, I had asked Maj. PN to call you and let you know of our well-being. He may have done that.

– Major Chandra Bhushan Dwivedi

24 May 1999

My love Bhawna,

Sweet kiss

I am doing well here and hope the same with you. Learned that you got your tickets to Muzaffarpur cancelled. Well, do make your future programme as per your convenience and judgement. We are all fine here and will continue to stay here for some more time. Do not get worried about anything at all.

We are sending Akhileshwar on leave on the 2nd of June. Will be sending Uma Nandan's warrant and one Form D, for you, along with him. So, use it in case you plan to go to Muzaffarpur.

Though I only had the pleasure of your company for 12 hrs, it was beautiful. We will meet again soon.

We keep meeting Maj. PN Prasad and Maj. Dua regularly. In fact, I had asked Maj. PN to call you and let you know of our well-being. He may have done that.

Maj. Rajender will leave for LGSC on the

26th of May. He too will speak to you over the phone.

With love,
Yours forever
Chandra.

Major Chandra Bhushan Dwivedi of 315 Field Regiment was my father. He was a leader who led from the front. He had a loving and caring nature and was hard to dislike. One day a nervous jawan heard a shell approaching and he jumped straight on to Daddy's lap in fear. It's hard for a soldier to act like this with a senior officer, but Major C.B. Dwivedi was not like any other officer. Instead of scolding him, he said to him, 'Beta, it's okay. It'll be fine.'

He had three daughters – his 31-year-old wife and his two daughters – waiting for him at home, but even an honest man like him was forced to paint a cleaned-up picture of where he was for his family. In his letters he rarely wrote about himself, but constantly worried about us. We had said goodbye to him already in the first week of

May and had headed to Siliguri, West Bengal, to our favourite cousins for our holidays. While we were making the most of our vacation, Daddy's unit had been deployed to Dras on 13 May. While my sister and I used to wake up in the morning to play in the river in those tough days of May 1999, he would take off every morning from his location, Pandras (village) in Kargil, to look for empty spaces around highways for parking the vehicles and artillery units coming into the war zone.

The only free time Daddy had was spent in staring at the map and devising plans for his regiment's next move. But he still wrote letters to us. He never forgot to do that.

It was the 1990s, and technology was not so advanced. Therefore the only way soldiers could regularly keep in touch with their families was by writing letters, which were sent via post. The Kargil war may be the last Indian war where soldiers wrote letters rather than send emails or WhatsApp messages.

It could take days before they'd get a reply from the other side, but the wait had become a part of their routine. Knowing you're fighting a war and that you may not live another day makes you feel deeply vulnerable. Exhausted by the fight they put up, cold and lonely, the soldiers could only express their vulnerability through their letters and their belief in God. Fortunately, every one of those soldiers believed in miracles. Their faith in God was evident in their letters.

If in case it is the will of God that I have to close my eyes from this place, please take care of dad and mum. They should be made to understand that I have been taken from this life to another better life.

– Captain Neikezhakuo Kenguruse

Daddy wrote to us every fortnight while he was at war, but the terrible truth was that most of the soldiers' families never knew whether their son/husband/father/brother was alive when they received his letters. Nor did we. We were busy catching a train when we lost Daddy; we heard the news one day after it had happened. This was after all a time when there were no mobiles and no Internet.

However, there were exceptions. There were soldiers who requested their commanding officers to make one call from the satellite phone to their family as their last wish, before they took their final breath. But chances were that as soon as the exchange would connect the two lines, the dreadful silence which followed on both sides would give away the horrific news of his martyrdom to his family.

Despite their feelings of vulnerability and loneliness, most soldiers never drew a true picture of what they were facing at war. They put on a brave face and wrote that everything was beautiful and 'normal' about the place they were at. It's so moving to learn that when faced with immense danger, all these men could think of was how to not get their loved ones worried. So these Indian soldiers learnt to lie, and to lie exceptionally well. And then they waited to be one of the lucky ones who could return home and apologize for their dishonesty.

~

Major Padmapani Acharya of 2 Raj Rif was a family man who knew his responsibilities well. He had left his pregnant wife Charulata behind, and all his thoughts were with her, their unborn child and their first child – their dog, Kaajal. Like all the other soldiers, he wrote to reassure his father, not even hinting at what he was going through.

3 June 1999

My dear Papa,

Thanks for your letter of May 25th. I hope this letter finds you hale and hearty. I am quite fine here and have escaped the boiling heat of the plains. It's pretty pleasant here.

We are indeed fortunate to be among the chosen few here and I will always try to live up to your ideals. Dubloo is not in my sector, but he is also part of the show. A great experience. (once in a lifetime types).

Papa, thank you for taking so much pains to bring us up despite all the odds. If it hadn't been for you and Ma, we would've been nowhere. All that we have achieved in life is due to your unstinting support all along the way. We shall not let down the family honour, come what may.

Too bad for Mr Krishnan. Please stand by Charu as you always have and help her get over the pain. I wish I had treated her better and been a better person. Please look after Kaajal. I keep thinking of her and imagining what she would be up to next. After all she's my first child. I shall always love her.

Take care of your health and do not overwork yourself. You have done enough already. Keep writing; it helps.

I have got all the winter clothing I need. There is no problem of any kind. I am happy here so don't worry about me. Dubloo would also be in good health. I love you Papa.

Yours affly

Babla.

Captain Neikezhakuo Kenguruse of 2 Raj Rif, on the other hand, was more honest with his brother about the danger he was in, but admitted to him that he couldn't tell his parents the harsh truth. He came from a family of warriors and, needless to say, a brave one at that. He was the Ghatak platoon commander during the attack on the Three Pimples ridgeline in Tololing on the night of 28 June. He voluntarily led his company on a cliff to attack a machine gun position of the enemy that was interfering with the battalion's main objective. He was injured after a splinter pierced his abdomen, but he didn't allow himself to give up and continued climbing. However, his boots kept slipping on the icy slope. Instead of retreating to get help, he decided to do something unbelievable. At a height of 16,000 feet and a temperature of −10 degrees Celsius, he took off his boots. Using his bare feet to get a firm grip, he eventually reached the top and demolished the enemy position with a rocket launcher.

2 Raj Rif
C/o 56 APO
8 June 1999

My dear brother,

How are you? How are you doing as a teacher? Liking it? Well, teaching is an interesting profession as you also keep learning new things each time you teach. I am also enjoying my profession here, commanding men and also leading them even to the worst of situations; a situation in which life and death is concerned.

I am sorry for not being able to talk to you properly. I thought you will be in Kohima that day throughout. I know you are also concerned about the things our family is facing, but do not worry. I will try my best and take care of things. I am sorry you have to look after yourself at this age even when you have an elder brother. I have already told dad and mum how much money I can send home. I have told them that it will be sent to the brothers and sisters through them. So please talk it out with dad and mum. I hope I will be able to live up to my commitment.

My dear brother, I don't know if Asenuo has already told you what I have told her. But please pay attention to what I am about to write now. I wonder if you are thinking of building your career in a better way. I don't mean to look down on your job, but the nature of your job is that you will remain what you are throughout. You need to build your image. I can tell you this that an officer may be drawing a lower pay than yours but will be respected more for his status. In other words, what he says will have greater impact on another person.

Remember this that there are lots of people who with your equivalent qualification are doing much better than you. It's not because you cannot do it but it is because you have never tried. I want you to grow in life.

Another thing that I want to tell you is about your relationship with both boys and girls. Remember this that your relationship must be healthy, both in front of Lord and man. You are no more a kid and so you should not jump around with the teenage kinds of relationships and infatuation. Your relationship should be based on true love and should have a future. You should have the approval of the family as well.

The last thing that I want to tell you today is about myself and the situation in which I am. There is nothing for you to worry. This is just to inform you so that everything works out later. I have already been shifted from Kupwara to Dras (Kargil sector) where there are lots of problems going on between India and Pakistan.

To tell you very frankly our lives over here are in danger throughout. I have not informed our parents about it because I don't want them to be worried. If in case it is God's will that I have to close my eyes in this place, please take care of dad and mum. They should be made to understand that I have been taken from this life to another better life. Take care of our brothers and sisters. Be an example to them. None of you should feel sad, and all of you should forgive me if I have done anything wrong. As for me, I have nothing against any of you. If I come back alive, I will tell dad and mum myself, but if I don't please tell them about Carmi, also do respect her for she is my best friend. She cares for me a lot. Remaining things I have written in my diary for dad and mum. Please check it out.

There is nothing for you to worry about. I have written this for your knowledge. It's a precautionary step I have taken so that nothing goes wrong even when I am no more. Take care of yourself and keep praying for me.

Your loving brother

Neibu

So many relationships, secrets and life lessons were left behind on torn and burnt pieces of paper. Those scraps, and the words they held, would later become prized possessions to some people for life.

~

Major Ritesh Sharma of 17 Jat had cut short his leave to be on the war front. His boys and, more importantly, his country needed him, and so he and many other soldiers like him voluntarily came back from their vacations to serve their countrymen in their time of need. Every soldier sought motivation during war and every decision made by every soldier mattered in war. One officer cancelling his leave or taking the lead in an assault when it was least expected of him acted as the driving force for every soldier to keep going, because they thought, 'If sir can, I should.'

With Rampal sir's and my arrival, everybody was really happy. In fact they were not expecting me to come back by 12-13th. But us coming back voluntarily was a good decision. Especially for

the jawans, they are even more motivated now.
– Major Ritesh Sharma

15 June 1999
1730 HOURS
OP Vijay

Respected Mom and Dad,

Sadar Charan Sparsh

Here, I am keeping well. I received both the letters you sent and news of how everyone is. Padam Sir got a little injured. Someone from here happened to call his wife Pooja and tell her that he was in the hospital, at which she got extremely worried and started crying. They had to get Padam Sir to make a call to her again from the satellite phone here to assure her that he was fine and she had no reason to worry.

We already knew that nothing was going to happen at this point. These days the position of the war is in our favour. We had a few failures initially, of which I got to know when I was still in Delhi.

Do not worry about me. This place too is my home and we all take care of each other.

I took lead of the mortar course. When the bombs started dropping on the enemy one by one, the soldiers rooted for me. You do not have to worry about how I am dropping the bombs on the enemy. We aren't too close. There's a good five km gap in between.

You were asking me about warm clothes. I have carried two combat uniforms and one set of warm uniform (in which we got our photograph clicked) in the bag I got in Jan. Except for that we have received some special clothing for the winters, including a warm jacket, sleeping bag, warm pants and socks. I bought a new pair of gloves. I got along a skivi too, the green one. All of this is more than enough.

I am at a high peak now. I eat my meals on time. The view here is picturesque. Snow-clad, tall, white mountains, with valleys under them and streams of cold water flowing too.

If Annu gets admitted in the 1PM batch too she can study at Lucknow along with Tanu. Tanu was also telling me that she doesn't have to do a job anyway. Our posting is not in the newspapers yet.

Let's see what happens in the coming days.
With Rampal sir's and my arrival, everybody was
really happy. In fact they were not expecting me
to come back by 12-13th. But our coming back
voluntarily was a good decision. Especially for
the jawans, they are even more motivated now.
In one of the issues of Outlook, where it says
'Undeclared War' at the top, it's our jawans who
are walking in the picture.

Okay ammi, I'll close this now.

– Maj. Ritesh Sharma

~

Captain Anuj Nayyar was Major Ritesh Sharma's
second in command and his friend. He had just
got engaged to be married and his parents were
beginning to plan his wedding. What they didn't
know was that he had left his engagement ring
with his commanding officer, Colonel Umesh
Singh Bawa, before going for the assault at
Pimple 1, because there was no certainty that
he'd come back.

The priorities of the determined Indian soldiers were set right – country, family, lover and then everything else, in that order.

13 June 1999

Darling Mom,

Got your letter dt. 8 Jun. So that little brat of mine has bought a Labrador, good! Send me some snaps.

Anyway, here all's fine. I'm enjoying myself. Don't worry. I'm being careful. Can't afford to be careless out here.

Things are cooling down a bit. Army is achieving good results.

Anyway, how's Dad's work coming along? He must be working day and night assured. What about Karan? Dad said he is not allowing Karan's Mandi trip. Why? C'mon let him enjoy himself. He's a big guy now. Let him get used to being responsible and on his own. Let him learn the ways of life first-hand.

Well, here I'm eagerly waiting for my car. Choice is Zen, Indica or Santro, whichever fits Euro II and I norms and fits in our budget.

I got to go now. Keep praying and remembering me. I promise I'll be very careful.

Love you four.

PS: Dad, that situation has yet to arrive which your son cannot face like Nayyar!!

No Fear ... Ever!!

Luv,

Anuj.

~

Captain Vikram Batra of 13 Jak Rif (Jammu and Kashmir Rifles) was confident that he would come back home with flying tri-colours. He had said to a friend before he left for the war, 'I'll either come back after raising the Indian flag in victory or return wrapped in it.' He was a passionate lover, a caring twin brother (to Vishal Batra [Kush]) and son, but before all that, he was a determined soldier. At war, his energy and passion were contagious, and it made him the face of the infantry in Kargil. He never got tired. It seemed like he had serious business to settle with the enemy personally and wouldn't stop till he got to the finish point.

23 June 1999

Dearest Kush,

Hi! Trust this letter finds you in the best of health and high spirits. Hope you've received my previous letter, which I wrote at Moni's add. I am writing you this letter from point 5140 (at Tololing) which you might be hearing about every day in the news. Yeah, you will be proud to know that we have captured it. Lt Jamwal (you met at Shimla) and I had gone to attack it and we captured it on 20th, killing 6 Pakis and captured hell lots of arms and ammunition. Whole battalion is very happy on our performance. We both have been recommended for MVC (Mahavir Chakra) for this task. And I have also picked up the rank of Captain.

Yesterday I had called up Mummy and Daddy from this place as we had got satellite phone for some time, so everyone got a chance to speak from wherever they were. I've also received letters from Nippy, Nippy's parents, Omkar. Rest everything is fine this end. Don't know about leave plan. Do give a call to Dimple and tell her about me that I am fine and tell her about my achievement also. We have got congratulatory calls from Army Chief, AG, DGMO and other army cdrs from all over.

Nothing more to write so I pen down. Do reply soon. I'm writing at a height of 17200 ft. Sorry for hand, as it's very cold here.

Love always.

Yours,

Luv!

Captain Batra was fearless, the kind of 'fearless' that could scare the enemy away; that's why he was called 'Sher Shah' by the Pakistani army. They had every reason to be wary of him. On 20 June, Captain Batra pounced on the enemy and killed four intruders in a hand-to-hand fight after secretly negotiating an almost vertical cliff to catch them by surprise. This he did knowing very well that he risked being spotted by the enemy. He was badly injured when he went on to recapture the peak of Point 5140 with his brave men from 13 Jak Rif, but until his last breath left him, he would not stop fighting. He would ask for a bigger challenge every time. '*Yeh dil maange more,*' he'd say to the journalists after every attack.

Fighting every day with little food and water but with inexplicably immense energy, the definition of 'normal' for every Indian soldier had changed. And yet it was the picture of the standard 'normal' that they communicated to their families.

At altitudes where there was hardly any oxygen, where one had to melt the blood-bathed snow around to quench one's thirst, where *shakkarpara* was the go-to food, only a superhuman could have thought of anything but his own survival. The Indian men in olive-green uniform were no less than supermen, but their concern to protect their families never left their souls. They had bodies of steel, but hearts of gold.

6

Victory or Death

Things turned around for the Indian side in June. On the 13th, after suffering many casualties, the army recaptured Tololing, a peak that seemed unattainable. It took days and several lives to shatter the confidence of the enemy. The show was finally over for the Pakistani side.

Captain Vijyant Thapar, aka Robin, of 2 Raj Rif, survived the toughest battle of the Kargil war and lived to tell the tale. Hardly out of the academy, he had risen to the position of 2IC (second in command, a position next just to the commanding officer) of his battalion. The brave boys of 2 Raj Rif had been the stars of Tololing.

Captain Vijyant Thapar was as crisp in his letters as he was in war. His sense of humour almost always prevailed over the circumstances around him. He made death seem easy, and maybe it was really that easy for him.

15 June 1999

Dear Mama, Papa, and Bindu

Hi, hope my letter finds you either reading or listening to the gallant act of 2 Raj Rif – the capture of Tololing.

1. I am alive till now, can't say till next attack
2. Life is tough
3. We are getting battle honour for it
4. My love to Mamaji
5. I am at 16,000 ft.
6. Lost one officer he might get PVC
7. Love Robin

It's a frustrating place. Snow all over myself in rocks, dead bodies lying to be picked up.

Got used to shelling now.

Preserve the newspapers of 14, 15, 16, 17, 18.

Love,

Robin.

~

Major Adhikari was one of the casualties of Tololing. He had just received a letter from his beloved wife. 'I want to read it in peace tomorrow after the operation is over,' he had said, stuffing his wife's letter in his pocket before going for the attack with his ten-men team to secure an initial foothold at Point 4590 on Tololing on 30 May.

The operation was regarded as almost impossible. The point the 18 Grenadiers had to capture was at a height of 15,000 feet, and the mountain face was almost 90 degrees steep. All the Pakistani soldiers had to do was push a rock from the top and the Indian soldiers would be finished. Despite his grievous bullet injuries, Major Adhikari continued to direct his men and even went on to charge a bunker, killing an enemy soldier in close combat. He didn't give up until his body succumbed to his injuries. But the fight was not over for him even after he had breathed his last. As he lay in full view of the enemy, they pumped his body with bullets.

It took many attempts before his body could be rescued. The letter from his beloved remained with him in his pocket, the letter he didn't know he'd never get to read.

Major Adhikari's extraordinary courage paved the way for the capture of Point 4590 and, eventually, Tololing.

~

Lieutenant Praveen Tomar of 2 Raj Rif was another of the survivors of Tololing. He wrote to his friend Gagan, also a soldier, a detailed account of one of the bloodiest battles in India that he was now witnessing. His account makes for one of the most powerful letters in this book.

25 June 1999

Dear Gagan,

1. It has been over a fortnight since I received your letter. But the nerve-wracking experiences and the hectic pace of events of the past few days forced me to wait for a few days before I could write to you. Anyway, thanks a lot for the letter. Even though your reply was a bit late in coming it could not have come at a more opportune moment.

2. By now you must have heard the name of Tololing Hill in Dras sector and that one of the Raj Rif Bro's took it. Well, we took it on night 12/13 June. My coy was the leading coy and I went in with the leading platoon. Before us 18 Grenadier had been tasked to capture and they had lost close to 20 chaps, including their 21C and one Major Adhikari, without success. The task was formidable indeed and our orders were explicit. Tololing had to be taken at any cost. We took the objective but the price my coy paid was a heavy one. My leading section was wiped out, everyone either dead or injured and the rest of my platoon is in tatters. It is a miracle indeed that I have escaped unhurt despite being in the leading party. People behind and even around me got hit while I kept having narrow escapes. I could see muzzle flashes at barely 5 metres but still came out safe. In fact I stepped on a stone that triggered a landmine. I fell down due to the blast but was safe otherwise. Seeing me fall people thought that I had lost my leg. So it came as a surprise for people in the base who received me the next day. Others were not so lucky as I

was. My coy lost 8 chaps including my coy cdr Maj. Vivek Gupta, one JW, my CHM, and 5 others. 12 of my men including my senior JCO are in MH.

It is not often that as an individual you write history for the whole army. But that fateful night Lt Tomar wrote history for the Indian Army. Congratulations are pouring in. The COAS has written in personally, Raj Rif centre commandant has written personally to each officer of the bn and I was quite busy talking to reporters and taking them around. I was interviewed by some foreign journalists and we are soon expecting a feature on our action in *India Today*.

But going to battle was a terrible and frightening experience. To motivate men to give their best, even their lives, while you fight your own inner fears. To put up a brave front in front of the men while inwardly you are yourself not so sure. To command men your father's age. You know that men will die but hope like hell it wouldn't be you. But when you fight all your fears are all gone, your doubts vanished. All you can think of is killing the enemy. They say baptism of fire is what makes you a man and it made me a man that night.

One fact that might interest you is that I had carried your letter into battle and that I was without food or water for 24 hours and was urinating blood due to my overexertion. But by God, we did it and we did it in style. Hope you are having a good time while I fight it out here. Please do find some time to write a few lines. It is very lonely out here and I can't even write home coz I don't want to trouble them. So please, please write a reply quickly.

Bye.

Yours,

Praveen.

The task was formidable indeed and our orders were explicit. Tololing had to be taken at any cost. We took the objective but the price my coy paid was a heavy one.

– Lieutenant Praveen Tomar

~

Of the many wins that were to come for the Indian army, it was Tololing that marked the turning point. There were more areas of their motherland to be recaptured and even tougher orders to give to the army teams. The next big win was Point 5140 on 20 June. It was one of the most arduous and crucial peaks in the Dras region.

The capture of Point 5140 created many more heroes and many more legends. One such hero, who firmly believed that 'a second gone in overthinking meant a step closer to failure', was Lieutenant Colonel Y.K. Joshi, the officiating commanding officer of 13 Jak Rif. He not only personally supervised preliminary actions but also got his hands dirty in the attacks, going far beyond his role.

During the assault at Point 5140, Lieutenant Colonel Joshi took to launching the Russian-made fagot missiles in broad daylight. His instructor training course came into use when the missile pilot got nervous that the missile might hurt the 13 Jak Rif men attacking the enemy bunkers on foot. But losing time was not an option for the Indian army. The place, timing and accurate moves were very crucial for them to win this fight.

To see Lieutenant Colonel Joshi fighting from the front was a great morale booster for his attacking troops. Therefore it's no surprise that one of his young officers was Captain Vikram Batra, the man who made Pepsi's tagline '*Yeh dil maange more*' a war cry with his undying conviction.

2 July 1999

Dear Kushu,

Hope you might have received my earlier two letters that I had written to you from battle zone only. So how's life? Hope you're enjoying at your place. That's really nice.

Regarding my side, I am fine here by the grace of almighty and busy fighting the war with the fools. Had come down for around 4–5 days for rest and recoup, but again moving up today for another offensive action. Can't write anything about that place because of security measures.

My bn is doing very well here. Earlier op I had undertaken myself and it was a great experience. Got 100% success. Was also interviewed by the press two days back – STAR TV, ZEE TV, NDTV and other personnel from different magazines and newspapers. So please look out for the newspapers as we are not getting a chance to see them here (*Statesman*, *Outlook* magazine, *Dainik Jagran* and others from 27 June onward, *India Today* also). Rest all is fine.

All set to go for the next op. Don't know when I will move down again. There's a good news, that instead of going to Shahjahanpur, our bn will be going to Gwalior now, but when it will be moving that is not fixed. Maybe after everything is clear here and that might take 2–3 months.

Convey my regards to Moni and Jija Ji, Hi to Sunny, Situ and Mona. Lots of love to you. Take care and God Bless.

Love always,

Do reply.

Luv.

In the battle of 5140, Captain Batra was badly injured, but that did not stop him from fighting.

And when he relayed '*Yeh dil maange more*' – his chosen code for success – to his command post, the whole country cheered with him. Always ready for the next challenge, the young hero eventually bid the country goodbye on 7 July while recapturing Point 4875.

After 5140, the next goal for the Indian army was to capture Knoll, located around the Three Pimples ridgeline in Kargil, where two *sangar*s could be seen. The assault on this area commenced on 28 June 1999, and 2 Raj Rif was chosen to lead the operations.

As Captain Vijyant Thapar and the soldiers of 2 Raj Rif charged towards the enemy bunkers, they received a shower of enemy artillery fire straight upon them. Fearlessly, Captain Thapar continued towards the enemy position, shouting '*Raja Ramchandra ki jai*', firing from the hip while throwing grenades. After engaging the enemy from a mere distance of fifteen metres for over half an hour, Captain Thapar decided to take one for the team. He surged ahead to put an end to the enemy, and while doing so, was hit by a burst of fire. Although he could not witness the victory that came on 29 June 1999, his platoon confirmed that it was the young twenty-two-year-old officer who had given a kick-start to that operation.

In the same attack, Major Padmapani Acharya, who was commanding a platoon that suffered 50 per cent casualties on their way to Knoll, also lost his life. Despite the many casualties and the dangerous positioning of his company, he valiantly led his team through artillery shells and small arm fire, ignoring the hail of bullets from the enemy position. He crawled up to the bunker and shoved grenades inside the enemy's *sangar*s. In this act of bravery, Major Acharya was seriously injured, but he had decided to protect his team of soldiers first. He ordered them to leave him alone and charge at the enemy under the fire support he provided. A night-long fierce battle ensued and it was only after the battalion had earned success, thus turning the course of the Kargil war, that Major Acharya finally closed his eyes.

This is how the country lost another of its bravest soldiers, a pregnant wife her beloved husband, an unborn daughter her father whom she would never see and an ageing couple a wonderful son.

15 May 1999

My Dear Charu,

I am in receipt of your letter of 03 May 99. Thanks a lot. I feel you write beautifully; you must write more often if your health permits.

I keep thinking of you all the time and the good and hard times we have shared together. Life is the best teacher and experience makes us all wiser. I am grateful to you for standing by my side through thick and thin, and making me a better person than what I was earlier. I would have not improved if not for you.

You have finally reached that state of womanhood where you will be creating, and moulding a new life. In creating a new life a woman is no less than a Goddess. For the baby, you would be the world. You must give the baby a healthy and happy world, and for that you must remain healthy and happy. Kaajal would require getting used to the baby since the beginning so that there is no jealousy and she gets used to looking after the baby like an elder sister. She can help a lot in generating confidence in the baby and make the baby grow faster. They should be the best friends for each other.

Today we had gone to the HQ to celebrate CO's 12th wedding anniversary. Thapar and myself presented him with a pair of ducks. They will be kept in the officers' mess.

Tell everyone at home that I am fine and I miss them like mad. Take care of your health and Kaajal's health.

Love,

Babloo.

Major Acharya had gifted his unborn daughter his life lessons, even though he could never gift her his company.

~

As June closed, the Indian army came closer and closer to their goal – to clear out the Pakistani army, peak by peak.

Lieutenant Manoj Kumar Pandey of 1/11 Gorkha Rifles put up a tough fight against stiff resistance from Pakistan's 8 NLI in Khalubar.

Amidst bullets flying over his head and grenades bursting around him, he destroyed four bunkers, thus inspiring his boys, before an MMG bullet hit his head. Not surprisingly, Lieutenant Pandey's platoon successfully recaptured the Khalubar ridgeline on 3 July 1999.

Some goals are so worthy, it's glorious even to fail.

– Lieutenant Pandey in his war diary.

19 June 1999

Dear Pawan,

(Do read this letter to as many as possible)

I received both your letters but could not reply to the first one. Both of them reached me in midst of hot battle. It's really difficult to fight the enemy at this altitude. He is well inside bunkers and defenses and we are in the open. He has planned his move very well and has occupied most of the heights. Initially things were very bad for us and we suffered many casualties but now situation is under control and more planned and deliberate attacks are going on. In last one and half months I've seen probably the worst in 'OP Vijay'; maximum casualties in the shortest time. I have myself brushed shoulders with death four times; but might be because of some good work I am still alive. Every day we are receiving letters from all over country saying same sentence 'Just do it'. It's good to see that at times of need and crisis our country gets united. I really don't know what will happen the next moment but till now I can assure you and all countrymen that certainly we would push back intruders; at whatever cost we have to pay; maybe our lives.

This operation has certainly given some exposure which cannot be quantified; like leading men in the face of death; their fear, their loyalty, the stress and strain both physical and mental which human beings can take; but yaar 'Indian Army' specially an infantry jawan is the ultimate. He would do anything provided he is led properly. As I have always told you, what infantry gives cannot be told, but today I'm so proud of my decision to join the 'Infantry' that I can't explain.

Here weather is cold but snow has started melting down. If sun comes then days are generally ok. Nights are cold with temperature −5 to −15 degrees.

It all would get over but time factor cannot be told, and frankly, no one can tell with certainty about his (enemy) going back. Just one request that guide my brother at this crucial moment of his life. (about his future)

Convey my regards to all your friends for being so considerate to us. Do remain in touch, it gives us a lot of moral support. If I come back we would have a lot of things to talk about, but certainly this is going to be an everlasting experience for me.

Yours,
Manoj.

It took many small attacks from all sides and many, many deaths to even come close to victory. Tiger Hill, one of the most strategic peaks in the entire region, was captured on 4 July after an eleven-hour battle.

Now I am the only one left, four are dead and Sooraj is out of action with two bullets in the hip. It has been a bitter struggle but I'm determined to fight till the finish.

– Lieutenant Praveen Tomar

~

As the war came to a close, the fight attained a fearsome intensity. For the Indian army, this would be their final push. On 4–5 July 1999, the responsibility to recapture two peaks, Pimple 1 and 2, was given to 17 Jat. It was a laborious attack; the battalion was allotted twelve artillery batteries for this task. Pimple 1 was successfully captured, and now 17 Jat's sights were on Pimple 2.

There were two kinds of officers in the Kargil war. One that commanded the troops to perfection, and the second that led by example. 17 Jat was full of the latter – soldiers who were leaders.

Major Deepak Rampal of 17 Jat led the attacks from the front on 4 July. They were given the task of recapturing Whale Back, a peak that gave the

Pakistani army full views of the Mushkoh Valley, Dras and Matayan.

During the move to launch the assault on Pimple 2, the company commander, Major Ritesh Sharma of the leading company, was injured heavily and had to be left behind. That was when his friend, Captain Anuj Nayyar, the company 2IC, led the assault. He cleared three *sangar*s that were coming in the way of the attack by firing a rocket launcher and lobbing grenades, without flinching at the fire that came his way. But as his company moved forward, Captain Nayyar got hit by an RPG round and died on 7 July 1999.

12 July 1999
Across Zojila at Bn Rear

Respected Mom and Dad,

Sadar Charan Sparsh

News is that I am perfectly fine here and you do not have to be worried with me in mind constantly. When we spoke on the call yesterday you seemed scared. By the time this letter reaches you, the fight might've ended.

We defeated the Pakistani 12 NLI Bn badly. The final blow to the enemy was given on Pimple 2 by my Charlie C coy. A splinter went through my right heel near the artillery shelling. It did not touch any bone and so I'm alright. It was good that it went through my foot or I would've had to go through an operation. Your courageous son did not return till he got all the other injured soldiers from the artillery shelling, gave them first aid and sent them back. I couldn't save the life of one of them, but I saved a dozen other injured ones. Only when my CO ordered me to come back and I was assured that Anuj would lead us to victory had I retired. But sadly, four hours after I left, Anuj had attained martyrdom. After this massive fight, the enemy knew where he stood and decided that backing off was the wisest thing he could do. You might've imagined the extent to which our army has made the nation and world proud through this victory by looking at the news coverage on Star News or *India Today*. It was only because of your blessings that were with me that an artillery shell blasted near me but I escaped. Please don't be more afraid after reading all of this. The fight is already over and our posting is out for Lucknow and we all will soon complete our 2 years and be back. Given the public hysteria that is developing, people will soon forget the soldiers again. When there was victory – the cavalier claimed it outright, the gunner boasted of his caliber, the signalmen and engineers published their worth, but the INFANTRY MAN stood silently with victory under his feet.

– Maj. Ritesh Sharma

~

'One day sir, I will supersede you,' Captain Anuj Nayyar of 17 Jat used to tease his senior officer, Major Ritesh Sharma. Circumstances forced him to take his senior officer's position and turn this joke into reality. And although Major Sharma joined his buddy in heaven in a few months' time, he spent every waking hour while he was at war trying to avenge his friend's death.

'Come back victorious. Never show your back to the enemy and do not become a prisoner of war or be declared missing,' Anuj Nayyar's father had said to him on the satellite phone, just a day before Anuj sacrificed his life for the nation.

22 June 1999

Dear Dad,

Got your inspiring letter dt. 14 Jun. Don't worry. I've yet to face an opponent who can win over me. That day can never come when I have to admit defeat. Fear was never in the dictionary you gave me as my Dad. Well, you are 200% right, the ground and air never hide anything. I've honed up my skills in the art of fighting with weapons, knives and bare hands too. Don't worry because nothing ever worries your son. Just worried about you five (Mom, you, Kannu, Timmu and Naughty). Take care of yourself and my gentleman Officer's promise, will celebrate your 25th Anniversary in Aug.

Dad, take care of Mani. I know she worries a lot. You too must be getting solid kicks for letting me join the army. Worry not. Your son is on your side always although I can't take your side openly against Mom. Bhai she's head of our family na!!

Take care and keep smiling … it always makes me smile.

Luv,

Anuj.

Young officers like Captain Nayyar didn't just pave the way for the big win in July 1999, they did it with big smiles on their faces.

When Captain Nayyar got hit, Captain Shashi Bhushan Ghildiyal of 315 Field Regiment personally led the assault with the shaken Jat soldiers, while also giving instructions to the artillery to destroy the enemy's *sangar*s. With this, the attack on Pimple 2 was successful, and at 1600 hours on 8 July, it had finally been captured from all sides.

But going to battle was a terrible and frightening experience. To motivate men to give their best, even their lives while you fight your own inner fears. To put up a brave front in front of the men while inwardly you are yourself not so sure. To command men your father's age. You know that men will die but hope like hell it wouldn't be you.

– Lieutenant Praveen Tomar

~

Raj Rif
C/o 50 APC
15 July 1999

Dear Gagan,

1. It was nice to receive your lovely card. Many thanks for the same. I have just one down after 10 days on 'Three Pimples'. The shadow of death still looms large over the place. I was feeling really down and depressed but your card worked wonders.

2. I am sure by now you must have come to know about our attack on 'Three Pimples'. The attack went on on the night of 28/29 June '99. If Tololing was bad, this was a bloody slaughter. You can imagine things for yourself when I tell you that we attacked from a side that was

declared unassaultable by the previous battalion. Just hours before the attack we came under fire by enemy arty. I myself had a very narrow escape when a bomb fell barely 5 metres away from me. Our RMO standing much farther got a splinter in his ankle and had to be evacuated while I got away without even a scratch. A day earlier a bomb fell right next to me but it did not explode. During the attack a bullet ricocheted off a stone and then off my helmet. The person next to me got hit twice while I got away both times. On Tololing things went to such an extent that there was a rumour that I had lost my leg in a mine blast. But lucky me I got away every time.

3. Unfortunately the others were not so lucky. The task was seemingly impossible but doing the impossible has become a habit with us. Maj. Acharya died leading the assault onto 'knoll'. Thapar took over and led from the front taking two enemy bunkers before a bullet through the head killed him. Neibu died while attacking from a sheer rock face. He got shot in the thigh but yet he kept climbing. He finally got a burst in his chest that flung him off the rock face into the

ravine 200 feet below. And yet we went ahead. For us there was no turning back, it was Victory or Death. We paid a heavy price but yes WE WON. They all died a soldier's death, leading from the front and fighting till the end. Such was the *josh* in the men that I was ready for an attack the very next day. Barely 3 hours before the H hour I was told to call it off and another battalion was sent in.

4. Life has been a long haul since Tololing. Of the seven officers that went in at Tololing only 3 are alive today. There were six of us here from 103 (Kalia, Thapar, Neibu, Sumeet Roy, Sooraj (Naushera tecko) and myself). Now I am the only one left, four are dead and Sooraj is out of action with two bullets in the hip. It has been a bitter struggle but I'm determined to fight till the finish. I have a score to settle with the Paki guys.

How are things at your end? Now that things are cooling down I don't think you will get employed. Best of luck for trg with ghataks. Practice hard, train hard and check everything, that is what I can tell you out of my own experiences. Before the attack we checked each weapon and equipment on ground. We even fired and tested our grenades. It was then that we came to know that a particular batch of fuses was faulty. They were changed and we saved a lot of men who may have suffered had their grenades not burst. Before Tololing we practised climbing and attacking in the dark on a hill similar to our objective. Every officer did 3 detailed recces in spite of the 7-hour arduous climb. Details were looked into and every contingency catered for. Our hard work paid dividends and the result is there for the whole world to see.

5. Things are quiet now but for some occasional shelling. Someone has told me that my name and photo has appeared in *India Today* and *Outlook* and that I have been quoted in some papers. I have been giving a lot of interviews lately to journalists, AIR, TV channels and even foreign news agencies. But the surprise was when I received letters from Raju, Khatri and even Harry. They are all doing well.

6. Do convey my regards to your CO and other officers. Take care and write back soon. Your letters make my day.

Yours,

Praveen.

PS: I am learning to type so please excuse my shoddy typing and the use of this rough paper. Anyway it gives you a chance to have a look at our special order of the day.

~

26 June 1999

Dear Maa,

Hope you and Baba are doing fine. Received your two letters in time, in fact I had been trying to call you up since long but there are no STD facilities here. So yesterday, I at last managed to get through an ESCON. The unit has been here since May 25, but I didn't tell you so because you would then unnecessarily get worried. We had some bad time initially, but now things have improved and we are having a lot of success. You must be reading about Tololing and point 5140 in the papers. Well, we were there at 5140 and participated in both the attacks.

We have been again tasked for another peak. Here, the weather is very warm but nights are pretty cold. The altitude varies from 10,000 to 18,000 ft.

My YO's was to commence from 15 July, but now it has been postponed for three months. I will be going in Sep/Oct. Before that I'll take one month of leave. How's the new house? Hope there are no problems there.

I'm putting my investment in DSOPF because the interest is 12%. I wanted to go for an LIC/ULIP. But right now there are no such facilities here. At present we are getting 'Best of Luck' cards from all over the country. Residents from 'Munirka Vihar' also sent us packets of dry fruits. So the morale is quite high. Rest is all fine here, don't worry. I am taking adequate care of myself and now I am one of the most experienced ones.

Take care and reply soon.

Lots of love,

Kutchi

Captain Sumeet Roy of 18 Garhwal Rifles was second in command during war. His 'D' company was responsible for recapturing point 4700 – a ridgeline where the Pakistan army had taken position after being evicted from Tololing. Going much beyond his call of duty, Captain Sumeet Roy personally assaulted the first *sangar* after a tough climb. After killing the enemies in the bunker, he planned to neutralize the enemy observation points nearby. He surprised the enemy by climbing up to their point without giving them a moment to rest. He killed the sentries and scared the others enough for them to leave large numbers of their arms and ammunition behind. He then went on further assaults without blinking an eye, till he was forced to succumb to his injuries on 3 July 1999.

~

Our soldiers had to look the enemy in the eye while charging towards them, but not once did they hold back. They kept going. With these final arduous battles, the winner was certain. The Indian army had brought their motherland to safety. The

Pakistani army began pulling out on 11 July, after the key peaks in Batalik were recaptured. The Indian army spent the next few weeks making sure the enemy had evacuated their premises while collecting their arms, ammunition and all their military storage. Operation Vijay was declared a success on 14 July by Atal Bihari Vajpayee and on 26 July, the Indian army announced that the Pakistani intruders had been completely evicted. As the heroes of Kargil searched for bodies and cleaned their guns, news headlines blared triumph all over India and the world. The soldier's job was done, for a while, at least. But now came the most painful part – saying goodbye to the dead. The count was 527 killed, 1363 wounded. The end of the war was more brutal than the actual war itself. There were letters, tears and, above all, guilt. A lot of guilt.

7

The Last Goodbyes

In some regiments, it's a tradition for soldiers to write a letter and leave it with their commanding officer before a tough assault. As painful as it may be, it is the only way they can express their last wishes, for that's all they might get. None of the soldiers mentioned below made it back home, but their words and emotions did.

For the families they left behind, all that remained were these letters and memories of their brave loved ones. The memory of the time the family had to cut short a vacation because the soldier had to leave for war. The memory of a phone conversation engraved deep in a daughter's mind, in which her father said to her without flinching, 'Beta, the weather here is very bad. Hence the disturbance.' The memory of the last time a soldier caressed his lover's hair with his strong, firm hands, and said confidently, 'Don't worry, I'll be back soon.'

Dearest Papa, Mama, Birdie, and Granny,

1. By the time you get this letter I'll be observing you all from the sky enjoying the hospitality of the Apsaras.

2. I have no regrets. In fact even if I become a human again I'll join the Army and fight for my nation.

3. If you can, please come and see where the Indian Army fought for your tomorrow.

4. As far as the unit is concerned the new chaps must be told about this sacrifice. I hope my photo will be kept in the 'A' coy mandir along with Karni Mata.

5. Whatever organ can be taken, should be done.

6. Contribute some money to orphanage and keep on giving 50/- Rs to Ruksana per month and meet Yogi Baba.

7. Best of luck to Birdie, never forget the sacrifice of these men. Papa you should feel proud. Mama, so should you, meet ***** (I

loved her) Mama Ji forgive me for everything wrong I did.

Okay then, it's time for me to join my clan of the Dirty Dozen. My aslt party has 12 chaps.

Best of luck to you all.

Live life king size.

Yours,

Robin.

~

20 June 1999

My Dearest Father and Mother,

I had never thought I will be writing a letter like this to you, but today I feel it is necessary to share my last message with you.

Pakistanis had infiltrated across the Indian border and had occupied some land, so we have moved to Dras and Kargil sector, near Jammu and Kashmir. Very soon I will be leading my men into the battlefield. I know God will be with me, he will protect me, but if God wants me to sacrifice my life here, I may not get another time to write to you again.

I am feeling very sad that I may not see you again, it is hurting me. But if God wants it that way, what can I do. I can't complain.

If I don't come back alive I want you to remember these few words of mine, dear Daddy and Mummy, I love you very much. I had always given my best to take care of you and I have always tried to please you. However, I could not succeed in this short span of life.

I have let you down in many ways, and I have troubled you in many ways. Please forgive me for all those mistakes.

Daddy and Mummy, you both have loved me so much and taught me to be a leader until the last day of my life. I am so grateful to you both. Thank you for all that you have done for me. May God bless you richly.

Dear Daddy, I am crying today as I think of my younger brothers and sisters. Please guide them to be good men and women. Tell them that I love them very much. Tell my Grand Pa and Ma that I love them. Give my regards to all our relatives and my friends and tell them to forgive me if I have done them any wrong in my lifetime.

Even if I tell you all to not cry when I die, I know you will all cry because you love me. But please comfort yourself and be happy again and with me in your memories even when I am no more.

Write to all my friends whose addresses are in my diary. Tell them I love them too. Dad and Mum I have to share this personal matter with you. I have a girlfriend, her name is Carmila (you must be knowing her too). I am afraid you may not like her. But I love her and she loves me too. This May when I came for holidays I asked for her hand and she agreed to marry me, so if I don't come back please take care of her too. She loves me too much and she is a true friend, we used to share our problems with each other. She loved me truly I know. So if I don't come back alive please do something for her. This is my humble request to you dear Daddy.

May the good God bless you richly, may the Almighty give you good health and peace of mind always.

Your loving son,

Neibu Kenguruse (Captain Neikezhakuo Kenguruse)

~

5 July 1999

Dear Kushu,

Sweet love & Hi there!

Received your affectionate letter yesterday only. I am writing at a very high altitude and ready for my luck. I might go up today in the evening. Two coys are already up and are engaged in a very heavy exchange. They are very near to the objective (about which I can't write you). I have written to you a letter two days back also at Moni's address. By the time this letter reaches you, you will have received that one. My interview had also come on STAR TV on 2nd July. There is a photograph of mine on the front page of the *Times of India* of 2nd July along with other members. Hope you've seen it and have recognized me. I'm having proper type beard now. As you've asked about the situation here, the situation is improving, but don't know how much time it will take, but our Army is doing a fantastic job here. Guys are really behind the bloody idiots.

Aare yaar! Don't take tensions, and keep doing your bit faithfully and sincerely, definitely God is looking at everyone and he will definitely reward one day. You've got all the potential to do anything and I'm sure you'll definitely rise very high in your life. Take life in its stride. You'll realize, you are the most happiest person. Rest everything is fine this end.

Convey my regards to respected Jija Ji and Moni, and to Sunny and C2 Bhaiyya and also to his fiancee, Hi to Mona and Deepika. Lots and lots of love to you. Take care and God bless.

Love always.

Do reply.

Yours,

Luv!

~

10 May 1999

Dear Mummy & Papa,

Jai Shri Hanuman Ji

I am writing this letter after a long gap. As I was away, not in contact with letters. So do not worry about me. I am perfectly fine at this place.

Mummy Ji how is your health. Hope you and Papa are fine. Vaibhav must be busy with his examinations. Tell him to write to me after his exam finishes.

Mummy how is everybody at Palampur? Hope all are fine. When is Montu's marriage? And how is everything at Amritsar? Hope Dadi Ji is fine.

Mummy say my hello to all at Amritsar, Shimla, Rehan and Suliali. Tell Masi Ji I will write to them when I will be able to be in contact with others.

Mummy also congratulate Sachin for his job. I hope all my friends have enjoyed Himanshu's sister's marriage.

Give my congratulations to Raju Bhaiyya and Shilpi Bhabhi to be blessed with a son. I will also write to them if above problem is solved. I have also written to Raman Uncle and Aunty. Papa how are Sodhis? Hope they are doing well at Nagrota.

Pari pana to Mamma. Tell her with her blessings I am doing well at this place.

Mummy rest is all fine. Hope Vaibhav and Papa are also fine. I'll try to call you if possible. Rest is all fine here. Snowing every day.

Your son,

Saurabh.

~

19 June 1999

Dear Papa,

Hope this letter finds you in best of health and spirits. Thanks for your letter and card dt 14 June '99.

We must understand that he would also be quite busy preparing for their share of the game. We are also already getting ready for our next task. Our unit now has to live up to the high expectations of the Army, Regt, as well as the media. You know what even the chief sent a letter of congratulations to the unit. It was indeed an honour for our unit to have been given such a task. Hard work and sound ethos does have its merits, don't you think? We now have to work harder to preserve the hopes and aspirations of our well-wishers.

Please don't worry about casualties. It's a professional hazard which is beyond our control, so why worry; at least it's for a good cause. In the Bhagvadgita Lord Krishna briefs Arjun on the following lines: '*Hato va prapyasi swargam, Jitva va bhokhyase mahima, taduthisht kauntaya, yudhaya kritnishchalaya*'.

No we are not air maint but food is good and we have a Bengali doctor if not Chinese. Yes the PMO Kargil visit was a good motivation. Good chap. I am quite a sight now with an unkempt beard and Vaseline cream all over my ugly face to counter the icy winds.

Please tell Manam that combat is an honour of a lifetime and I would not think of anything less. What better way to serve the nation. I am proud I'm in the Infantry and especially in our illustrious battalion.

Take care of your health as well as Manam's. Don't worry and lose sleep. Tell a story a day of the Mahabharata to Charu, so that your grandchild imbibes good values.

Jai Mataji Ki

Yours affly,

Babloo.

~

30 June 1999

My Love Bhawna, Sweet kiss.

We are fine here. Received your letter and learnt of the news upon reading it. Do not think too much about this place or get worried. Whatever you watch on TV is not always true, a lot of it is made up as well. Have faith in God almighty, we will be back soon.

How was the wedding as also the trip to Siliguri? Do write to me about it.

Both Capt. Durani (the one from 891) and Maj. RK Malhotra are around this area and remember you often. 158 Med., that was in Meerut, is here as well. Two of their officers' families are staying in SN Park as well. I speak to Col. SP Singh almost every day. Do let Mrs SP know that he is doing well.

Do write to me every chance that you get. Make sure to hire a tutor for Neha. Where is Pandit ji's family now? Are they shifting or not? If possible, you could hire his daughter for tuitions as well. How's Monu boss doing? She must be back from Bombay by now. When is she getting married?

More in next letter. Take good care of yourself!

With love,

Yours forever

Chandra.

~

Dear Maa,

Hope you are keeping fine and so is Baba. I am fine here and getting along with my duty well. You must have read in the papers about the capture of point 4700. You'll be proud to know that I led the attack and successfully captured pt

4700 and another adjoining feature. Since then we have successfully captured the other features and have been getting features in the papers and radio news every day.

There is another proud moment in store as I have been recommended for a gallantry award, to be declared on 15 Aug '99. At present I am having a very good time in the bn in terms of respect and reputation, as so far I have led my company into three successful attacks i.e. on 5140 and 4700.

Our unit move has been confirmed to Jamnagar by Feb 2000. So, the advance party will leave by Feb. My YO's is now rescheduled for Oct 15.

How is Bapi? By now he must have come back from his YO's and must be availing his leave. You can tell him to keep the notes etc at Delhi, so that I can collect them prior to my YO's.

How's your job & classes going on? Hope Baba is keeping fine nowadays.

I shall try for leave prior to my course in Sept, but nothing is certain so far.

Don't worry about me. I am taking adequate care of myself.

Nothing to worry about from my side.

Take care and write soon.

PS: Cleared all my part B exams.

Love,

Kutchi

~

Often during war, artillery units had to make a tough choice and decide if an operation would go on through the night, because gunfire in the dark could give away the regiment's position to the enemy. And without artillery support, infantry assaults were next to impossible.

It was 2 July 1999, and the battle for Tiger Hill had begun. 315 Field Regiment was in a dilemma at Pandras, the location that Major C.B. Dwivedi had picked for the unit to pitch their tents. Should they continue firing at the enemy position or should they stop? In the latter case, the infantry units (18 Grenadier and 8 Sikh) would've been in serious danger. Daddy, being the officiating second in command, chose the former and riskier option because without artillery fire, infantry assaults were dangerous and incomplete.

He rushed out of his tent and motivated his boys to keep firing, to keep at it. He knew how difficult it would be to get through this, but he had to make the tough choice. It was either protecting himself and his men or protecting a whole unit of foot soldiers – he chose the latter option. It's the madness in a soldier's blood that most of us will never understand. He was mad.

He sat at the gunner's position and continued firing at the enemy. At that moment, a shell landed right next to him. As soon as he heard the shell coming, he asked all his boys to enter their tents. While screaming '*Andar jao*' at the top of his voice, he forgot to run for his own life. It was too late, and he was hit on the arm. But what he didn't realize was that fragments of the shell had also pierced his body. In the heat of war, a soldier doesn't feel pain. Maybe that was the reason he told the doctor that he was doing fine. He suffered a lot of internal bleeding but wasn't aware that it wasn't just his arm that was injured. Tiger Hill was almost the last stop for the Indian army, and my father missed seeing the tricolour waving atop it by two days.

The heroes of 315 Field Regiment received the honorary title of 'Kargil', but could never get the accolades that were reserved for the infantry. Artillery was the backbone of Kargil, but it wasn't the glamorous face of the war. But Daddy and all the soldiers who have not been heard of, who gave an arm and a leg fighting for this country, were an essential part of this glorious victory, and no one can take that away from them.

~

Duty knocks on your door in the most unexpected of ways. When your son or brother or husband or father leaves you behind for the country and never comes back, you find yourself caught in a storm of emotions. You're angry but you're proud, you want to cry your lungs out but you also want to keep a brave face on, you are resentful at the cruel hand fate has played but you know you have to put up a dignified front. After all, it runs in the blood . . .

or that's what they say.

> 'Don't cry, you're a martyr's kid.'
> 'Stand for your rights, you're a martyr's wife.'
> 'You gave birth to a brave soldier, you should
> be proud and not sad.'

There's no other way. At least, no other socially acceptable way of 'acting' like a martyr's family. It takes years for the contradictions to smooth out, for you to feel the right emotions and act the right way. And that's when a sense of pride slowly starts to overpower the feeling of loss. That's when you read that letter again, the letter that reminds you of the man who gave his tomorrow for your today, happily.

13 June 1999

My Sweetheart,

Sweet kiss.

We are all fine here and hope the same with you.

Just received your letter yesterday, the one you sent to Meerut. We'll reach Meerut on

3rd July. Please keep writing letters to us, now these are my only support. How is your health? Please take care of yourself. Remember, health is wealth. If you'll be healthy, only then will you be able to do your work properly.

We are here waiting for you, please always keep this in mind. Everyone is fine at your home as well.

Eagerly waiting for your next letter.

With lots of love,

Yours and only yours,

Bhawna.

~

12 June 1999

Dearest Daddy,

How are you? I am fine here and hope the same with you too. I received two of your letters, but it seems that you have not received my letter. I was very happy to know that leaves have come on the rose plants. I have told mausaji to bring the camera, as per your instructions. Are the conditions in Kargil improving or getting worse? When are you all coming down? I and Diksha had a recitation competition which was house-wise. We had four groups, of classes – 1 & 2, in this our house came first. 3 & 4, in this also our house came first and Diksha came first. 5 & 6, in this our house came second and 7, 8 & 9, in this our house came first and I came third. Overall our house was first and we and our house incharge were really happy.

More next time. I know you have no time to write letters but if you get some time, please write a two-line letter. Take proper care of yourself.

With lots and lots of love for my loving daddy.

Your loving daughter,
Neha

~

12 June 1999

Dear Daddy,

How are you? We are fine here and hope the same with you.

Mummy has still not bought my green jeans. Please tell her to buy it. You again wrote letters to only Neha di, I've even started calling her didi. Now you should be happy and come back home.

See you soon!

Love,

Diksha.

List of soldiers mentioned
in this book

Captain Saurabh Kalia (1976–99), survived by Dr N.K. Kalia (father)

Captain Amit Bhardwaj (1972–99), survived by Mr O.P. Sharma (father)

Major Rajesh Singh Adhikari, MVC (1970–99), survived by Mrs Kiran Adhikari (wife)

Major Chandra Bhushan Dwivedi, SM (1961–99), survived by Mrs Bhawna Dwivedi (wife)

Captain Manoj Kumar Pandey, PVC (1975–99), survived by Mrs Mohini Pandey (mother)

Captain Anuj Nayyar, MVC (1975–99), survived by Mr S.K. Nayyar (father)

Captain Vikram Batra, PVC (1974–99), survived by Mr G.L. Batra (father)

Major Padmapani Acharya, MVC (1968–99), survived by Mrs Charulata Acharya (wife)

Brigadier Umesh Singh Bawa, VrC, SM (Retd) (1958–2014)

Colonel Deepak Rampal, VrC (1965–present)

Major Ritesh Sharma (1975–99), survived by Mr Satya Prakash Sharma (father)

Lieutenant General Yogesh Kumar Joshi, AVSM, VrC, SM (1962–present)

Colonel Shashi Bhushan Ghildiyal, VrC (1974–present)

Captain Sumeet Roy, VrC (1977–99), survived by Mrs Sapna Roy (mother)

Captain Neikezhakuo Kenguruse, MVC (1974–99), survived by Ngseue Kenguruse (brother)

Colonel Praveen Tomar, SM

Military terms referred to in
the letters and text

Coy:	Company
Bn:	Battalion
Mortar:	A short smooth-bore gun for firing shells (technically called bombs) at high angles
Sentry:	A soldier stationed to keep guard or to control access to a place
CO:	Commanding Officer
2IC:	The second in command (2IC) is the officer in line to lead the regiment in the absence of the commanding officer
Sangar:	A small protected structure used for observing or firing from, which is built from the ground

Foot soldier:	Infantryman
LGSC:	Long Gunnery Staff Course
DSOP:	Defence Services Officers Provident Fund
CHM:	Company Havaldar Major
JCO:	Junior Commissioned Officer
MH:	Military Hospital
RMO:	Regimental Medical Officer
COY CDR:	Company Commander
RPG:	Rocket-Propelled Grenade
Aslt:	Assault
Senior subaltern:	Senior officer
Op:	Operation
MMG:	Medium Machine Gun
Regt:	Regiment

Acknowledgements

I was very tempted to make this a five-page-long thank-you speech because this book was hard in so many ways, and without these people who have helped me, my first book would've never seen the light of day. But I was quick to realize that I need you to read this book fully, so I'll keep this very short.

Major General Yogesh Kumar Joshi, thank you for reminding me of Daddy. I know if he were around today, he'd look and behave exactly like you.

Colonel Deepak Rampal, thank you for iterating and reiterating the fact that we're in this together, and for proving it every step of the way.

Lieutenant Colonel Amit Aul, thank you

for giving me the young officer's perspective during war.

Gaurav C. Sawant, thank you for making it possible for me to look at the Kargil war from the lens of a journalist.

Vikas Manhas, thank you for keeping the martyrs' stories alive in our hearts and for helping me in every way you could.

A thank you is not enough for every martyr's family members who trusted me blindly with the most prized possessions of their lives. I'll cherish every bit of conversation I had with each of you; thank you for reliving the toughest days of your lives with me.

Thank you Trishant Srivastava for translating some of the most important lines in this book from Hindi to English.

A big thank you to Daddy's regimental officers and course mates who have always been available during these eighteen years to fill the tiny gap in the war stories that Daddy left behind. Especially Colonel Sunil Upadhyay and Colonel Shashi Bhushan Ghildiyal, thank you for everything.

Finally, thank you my two mothers, Bhawna

Dwivedi and Neha Dwivedi, for being the sole reason for everything I am today and everything I will be in the future. And my brother-in-law Major Rohin Chhibber, for keeping the family's legacy going.

A very special thanks to my extended family who made sure through these nineteen years that we never felt Daddy's absence in the most important events of our lives. It's important to mention my father figure and my brother here, Dr Tanuj Siddhartha, for being the support I absolutely can't do without in the career path I've chose for myself in this lifetime. I still remember what you said to me that day, 'Beta, God only calls good human beings to himself.'

Writing this book needed a lot of emotional support and I can't thank Prashansa Sharma enough for always being my pillar of strength.

Lastly and most importantly, Chiki Sarkar, my editor and publisher, thank you for making me write and rewrite this book. The pressure was worth it!

juggernaut

THE APP FOR INDIAN READERS

Fresh, original books tailored for mobile and for India. Starting at ₹10.

juggernaut.in

1

CRAFTED FOR MOBILE READING

Thought you would never read a book on mobile? Let us prove you wrong.

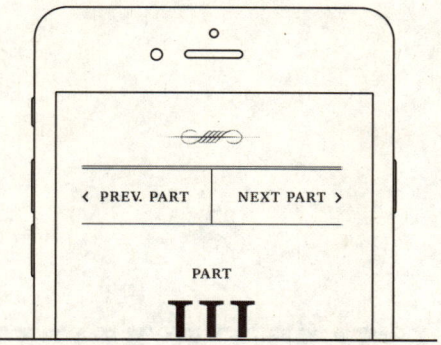

Beautiful Typography

The quality of print transferred
to your mobile. Forget ugly PDFs.

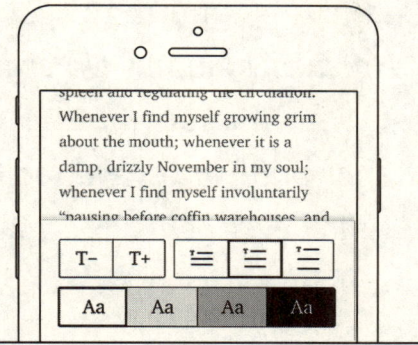

Customizable Reading

Read in the font size, spacing
and background of your liking.

AN EXTENSIVE LIBRARY

Including fresh, new, original Juggernaut books from the likes of Sunny Leone, Praveen Swami, Husain Haqqani, Umera Ahmed, Rujuta Diwekar and lots more. Plus, books from partner publishers and loads of free classics. Whichever genre you like, there's a book waiting for you.

DON'T JUST READ; INTERACT

We're changing the reading experience from passive to active.

Ask authors questions

Get all your answers from the horse's mouth. Juggernaut authors actually reply to every question they can.

Rate and review

Let everyone know of your favourite reads or critique the finer points of a book – you will be heard in a community of like-minded readers.

Gift books to friends

For a book-lover, there's no nicer gift than a book personally picked. You can even do it anonymously if you like.

Enjoy new book formats

Discover serials released in parts over time, picture books including comics, and story-bundles at discounted rates. And coming soon, audiobooks.

4
LOWEST PRICES & ONE-TAP BUYING

Books start at ₹10 with regular discounts and free previews.

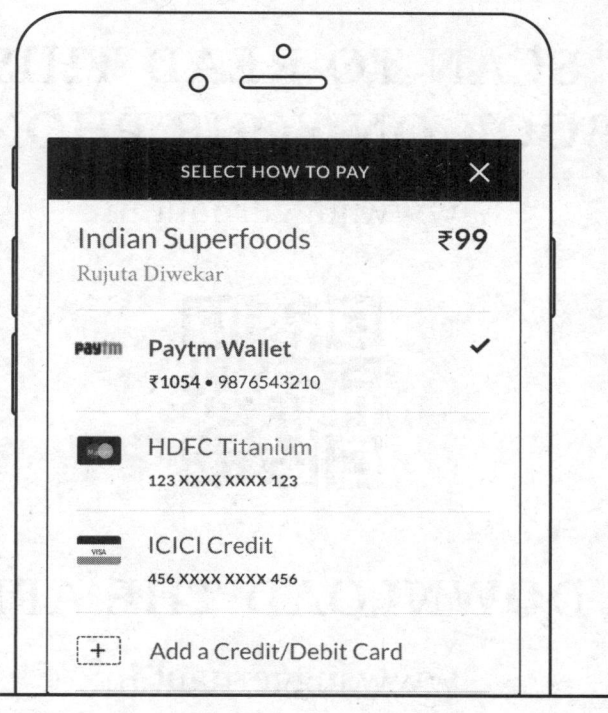

Paytm Wallet, Cards & Apple Payments

On Android, just add a Paytm Wallet once and buy any book with one tap. On iOS, pay with one tap with your iTunes-linked debit/credit card.

Click the QR Code with a QR scanner app
or type the link into the Internet browser
on your phone to download the app.

SCAN TO READ THIS
BOOK ON YOUR PHONE

www.juggernaut.in

DOWNLOAD THE APP

www.juggernaut.in

For our complete catalogue, visit www.juggernaut.in
To submit your book, send a synopsis and two
sample chapters to books@juggernaut.in
For all other queries, write to contact@juggernaut.in